MARIA MONTESSORI

The Italian doctor who revolutionized education for young children

by Michael Pollard

MOREHOUSE PUBLISHING
Harrisburg, PA • Wilton, CT

MARIA MONTESSORI

by Michael Pollard

Picture Credits
AMI, Amsterdam — 12, 13; AMI, London — 23, 30-31, 45, 47, 50, 54, 55; Nick Birch — 44, 56-57; Bridgeman Art Library
— 10-11, 14, 19; Giancarlo Costa — 17; ET Archive — 53; Mary Evans Picture Library — 8, 17, 26 (above); Fine Art — 11;
Hulton — 42; The Mansell Collection — 16, 20; Military Archive — 53; Jean Miller — 48; Montessori Training Organization,
India — 60; Moro Roma — 7, 9, 21; David Kahn, NAMTA/Waltuch Collection — 32, 37; Nienhuis — 41, 45; Popperfoto —
4, 28, 34, 58, 59; Preschool Book — AJine D. Wolf, 38, and Jean Miller, 48; Roger-Viollet — 24; Scala — 6, 14, 18, 23, 27; ©
SUPERSTOCK — 67; The Tate Gallery, London — 26 (below); Aline D. Wolf — 38.

The publishers would like to thank the AMI (Association Montessori Internationale), both in London and Amsterdam, for its
generous assistance in text and picture research on this book.

North American paperback edition first published in 1990 by **Morehouse Publishing**

Corporate Office
P.O. Box 1321
Harrisburg, Pennsylvania 17105

Editorial Office
78 Danbury Road
Wilton, Connecticut 06897

First published in the United Kingdom in 1990 with an
original text © 1990 by Exley Publications Ltd.
Additional end matter © 1990 by Gareth Stevens, Inc.

Library of Congress Cataloging-in-Publication Data

Pollard, Michael, 1931-
    Maria Montessori / by Michael Pollard.
      p.   cm. — (People who have helped the world)
    Reprint. Originally published: London : Exley Publications, 1990.
    ISBN 0-8368-0217-9
    1. Montessori, Maria, 1870-1952—Juvenile literature. 2. Educators—
Italy—Biography—Juvenile literature. 3. Montessori method of education—
Juvenile literature. I. Title. II. Series.
LB775.M8P65
370'.92—dc20   [B]   1990   89-49417

Gareth Stevens ISBN 0-8368-0217-9 (lib. bdg.)
Morehouse ISBN 0-8192-1539-2 (softcover)

Series conceived by Helen Exley
Series editor, U.S.: Rhoda Irene Sherwood
Research editors, U.S.: Kathleen Weisfeld Barrilleaux and John D. Rateliff

Printed in Hungary

1 2 3 4 5 6 7 8 9 96 95 94 93 92 91 90

Opposite: The last decades of the nineteenth century in Italy were a period of rapid urban and industrial growth. Attracted by the prospect of work in the new factories, Italians flocked to the cities. Their rewards included grossly overcrowded, low-grade housing and grueling work in poor conditions for little money. These tenements are typical of the conditions in which Maria Montessori began her work in Rome in 1907.

San Lorenzo

They were children of the slums. They were poorly fed, uncared for, and terribly pale from lack of sunlight and fresh air. Some were shy and sullen; others were crying.

They shambled along. Their heads were down and their eyes were dull. They seemed like prisoners without hope. So far, their lives had brought them nothing but misery, pain, hunger, and fear. Why should today be any different?

They were the children of San Lorenzo, a district then on the edge of the beautiful city of Rome, in Italy. They lived in apartment blocks that they had steadily vandalized — scratching and kicking the walls, fouling the stairways, and breaking anything that could be broken.

While their parents were at work and their older brothers and sisters were at school, these small children, aged between three and six, were shut out of their homes and left to wander about the neighborhood until evening.

But not today, January 6, 1907. Something new was happening in San Lorenzo. The owners of the apartments had decided to collect the young urchins together in a room and pay someone to look after them while their parents were at work.

This would be cheaper than paying constantly for repainting and repairs. Today was opening day for the new room.

The children came because they were told to. They weren't excited or even curious. Nothing exciting or interesting had ever happened to them before. They didn't know what it was to be excited or interested in anything. As far as they knew, there was no reason why things should change.

But they were wrong.

"They were tearful, frightened children, so shy that it was impossible to get them to speak. Their faces were expressionless, with bewildered eyes as though they had never seen anything in their lives. They were indeed poor, abandoned children, who had grown up in dark, tumbledown slum-dwellings, with nothing to stimulate their minds, and without care. . . . It was not necessary to be a doctor to recognize that they were in urgent need of food, open air life and sunlight."
Maria Montessori, in
The Secret of Childhood

The Casa dei Bambini

The children came wearing stiff, blue, uniform smocks of the kind given to children who lived in poorhouses, special houses for people who had no money or secure jobs. They were told to hold hands, and an adult pulled one child forward so that the others had to follow.

The children wondered what was going to happen. Had they done something wrong? Were they going to be punished? Were they going to be taken away? They did not expect good news. There had been no good news in the lives of the children of San Lorenzo.

The children knew only one of the people in the room. She was Signorina Nuccitelli, whose father was caretaker of one of the apartment blocks. Standing with her was another woman, young and pretty, with fine chestnut hair, wearing a dark dress. In front of them were small tables with chairs to match. A tall cupboard stood in one corner.

Many artists who tried to record conditions in the slums of Italy were unable to bring themselves to tell the truth. This picture, Three Children, *by G. Esposito, gives an idealized view of what childhood was like for the poor children of the city streets. A more realistic painter would have shown the marks of disease, hunger, and neglect on the children's faces.*

It was the young woman in the dark dress who stepped forward once the frightened children had stopped crying and sniffling. "My name is Dr. Montessori," she said. "Welcome to the Casa dei Bambini [the Children's House]."

Training

Dr. Maria Montessori had liked the name *Casa dei Bambini* when it was first suggested to her. It was no accident that the room was furnished with child-sized tables and not with school desks. Dr. Montessori wanted the room to look as unlike a school as possible because what she planned to do there was quite different from what happened in school.

In Italy at that time, and in every other country, schools were places where children were trained rather than taught. Lessons involved learning things by heart and reciting them in parrot fashion after the teacher. Children who didn't learn fast enough were frequently beaten for "laziness."

There were only a few books for them to read, with no maps or pictures, and often no writing materials. The children sat up straight at their desks and were not allowed to move unless they were told to. Talking was forbidden. Any child who was interested enough in a lesson to ask the teacher a question about it would be told to be quiet. There was no opportunity for children to find things out for themselves.

The idea of education then was that the teacher had a certain amount of knowledge to pass on, and the children must learn it word for word. No one thought that going to school could — or should — be enjoyable or interesting. Children were there to be trained for adult life, and the sooner they were trained well enough to do a job, the better. Meanwhile, they must be quiet and, above all, obedient.

Choice and discovery

Maria Montessori was not a trained teacher, although she had studied theories of education. So when she began thinking about how young children should learn, she had none of the fixed ideas that teachers had. Maria had previously worked in institutions with children who had disabilities of one kind or another.

In reality, the lives of city children were desperately unhappy. Ill-fed, poorly clothed, and uncared for, the children lived without hope from day to day. Their contacts with authority — such as the painful and humiliating process of delousing shown here — were mostly unpleasant. Maria Montessori brought into their world not only sympathy and under-standing, but also concern for their future.

They had been placed in institutions to keep them out of the way of the rest of society. Most of the children were mentally retarded or emotionally disturbed, or had learning disabilities of some kind, so people regarded them as impossible to educate.

But Maria had proved them wrong. Instead of using the usual teaching methods, over time she developed special materials that allowed the children to use their senses as a means of learning. The children were encouraged to learn by exercising their senses of touch, sight, smell, and sound. This way, Montessori enriched their educational experience and, in fact, helped some to reach the same standards and pass the same exams that children did who were of normal intelligence.

Maria's methods of teaching with unusual smells, with rough and smooth tactile experiences, and with bright geometrical and mathematical shapes had proved to be successful with the children in the institutions. Now she was looking for a chance to try them with children who had no disabilities.

The invitation to set up a children's house at San Lorenzo was the opportunity she had been waiting for. But she was not able to give the project all her attention because she was a full-time lecturer at the University of Rome.

So Candida Nuccitelli, the caretaker's daughter, looked after the day-to-day running of the Children's House. As often as she could, Maria looked in to help and to observe what was going on.

Maria had ordered sets of learning materials for the San Lorenzo children. These materials were based on those that she had used with the children who had disabilities. As people began to understand Montessori's teaching techniques, these materials became known as the "didactic apparatus." They were designed to enable the children to correct themselves by trial and error.

The vital principle Montessori pushed was that the children find answers to questions by themselves. She instructed Candida *not* to teach the children. Candida was simply to look after the children while they chose their own activities and found out for themselves what could be done with the materials.

Opposite: Teaching and learning in a school in 1875. This style of teaching was aptly known as "chalk and talk." It is hardly surprising that the students lost concentration and learned little.

For many Italian children, there was no school at all. The official age for leaving school was twelve, but the law was often ignored. As a result, in 1901, fewer than half of the people of Italy could read or write.

Above: The Naughty
Schoolchildren _was the
title the artist gave to this
picture. One girl is being
fitted with a dunce's cap.
Another is kneeling in front
of the teacher as a
punishment. A third is
asleep. There is very little
in this classroom to excite
or interest the pupils._

Start of a revolution in education

In the majority of countries today, when children go
to school for the first time, they are usually allowed
— in the beginning — to choose their own activities.
In 1907, it was almost unheard of. It was the opposite
of what every teacher had been trained to do.

The opening of the first Children's House at San
Lorenzo on that January morning was the start of an
educational revolution that was to spread in time and
affect everyone who has been to school in the past
sixty years. It would also change the way adults
understand children and how children learn and even
the kinds of toys young children are given to play
with at home.

In 1907, Maria Montessori was thirty-seven years
old. She was already well known within Italy as a
doctor, a lecturer, and a campaigner for women's

Left: A Roman carving of teacher and pupils. By the nineteenth century, little had changed. The teacher's job was to talk, and the students' was to listen. In this way, knowledge was passed on from one generation to the next without ever being questioned. Students were given little opportunity to make discoveries by themselves or to think things out for themselves.

Maria Montessori in 1880, when she was ten. Although she did not, at this age, shine academically, she had already acquired some of the aspects of her character that would motivate her life. It was at this age, when she was very ill, that Maria said to her mother, "Do not worry. . . . I cannot die; I have too much to do." She already held strong beliefs and had a forceful way of expressing them.

rights, but the work she began at San Lorenzo was to make her famous throughout the world.

Hers would become a leading name in the history of modern education. For the rest of her life and long after, people would admire her and follow her. In time, they would also argue about her techniques and ideas about learning.

Maria's ambition

Maria Montessori was born on August 31, 1870, in the small town of Chiaravalle in eastern Italy. She was the only child in the family. Her father, Alessandro, was a former military man and a successful government finance official for the tobacco industry. When Maria was just five, the Montessori family moved to Rome, and a year later she started school.

In her early years at school, Maria did not stand out from other children. But even as a child she possessed a great driving ambition. She was a powerful character with a strong sense of duty and an assertive nature.

This would make her unpopular with some people but successful with others. She decided very early on that she did not want to be a teacher when she grew up. As a young girl, she dreamed of being an actress.

Math or marriage?

This changed when she was twelve. At that age, in Italy, children could leave school and go to work. But if they stayed in school for more training, they began to specialize in different subjects.

Most girls expected to get married and have children or, possibly, to teach. So they took courses in the classics. In these courses, they learned Latin, Greek, and literature.

But Maria grew interested in mathematics — an interest that stayed with her for life — and wanted to be an engineer. Such a choice was unusual for girls, so she had to attend a boys' secondary school.

Because the school did not cater to girls in any way, there were no facilities for Maria and the other girl students. During breaks it was thought improper for the sexes to mix on the playground, so the girls were kept in a room, to protect them from the boys!

As in other schools, study meant learning facts by heart and chanting them back to the teacher in daily "drills." This does not seem to have discouraged Maria, although the monotony of this method of learning was to influence her later in her life.

Her outstanding intelligence and interest in scientific subjects overcame the deadly dullness with which they were taught. She passed her exams with high marks, and in 1886, at sixteen, she went on to a technical college.

Rift

Family ties and traditions are very important to the Italian people, and most parents want their daughters to be happily married and the mother of a growing family. But until the time comes for their daughter to be married, families want to protect her from the attention of boys — wanted or unwanted.

There would have been serious trouble for Maria if, for example, someone from the family had seen her even talking to a boy from school.

Maria was an attractive girl, and her parents could have expected her to marry well. She might have married into one of the families of merchants or government officials who were their friends.

But Maria made an unprecedented decision that would cause some disagreement within her family — she decided she wanted to become a doctor. No woman in Italy had made this decision before.

This choice was to cause a terrible rift between Maria and her father. The two of them had very different ideas as to what her future should be and, at first, these ideas were irreconcilable.

It was not until Maria was speaking in public, becoming well known, and earning praise that Alessandro and Maria were able to make up their differences. Maria was successful in a previously unheard-of way for a woman.

Maria's mother, Renilde, was from an academic family and a woman caught between the old and the new ways in Italy. This caused her to push Maria into doing all that she wanted. She had hoped for, and wanted to do, many of the things Maria was making possible for women.

Maria, at age seventeen. At this time, she was at technical school and her love of mathematics was leading her to a scientific career. Her first choice was engineering. This was an unusual ambition for a young Italian woman, and it began a rift between Maria and her father which lasted for several years.

Above: This was the kind of life that most middle-class Italian girls grew up to expect and that Maria Montessori rejected: a "good marriage," children, quiet conversation in the café, then home to domestic duties.

Right: Working in the dissecting room — an essential part of medical training — horrified Maria. Working with dead bodies distressed her, the more so because she was allowed to work in the room only after the male students had left.

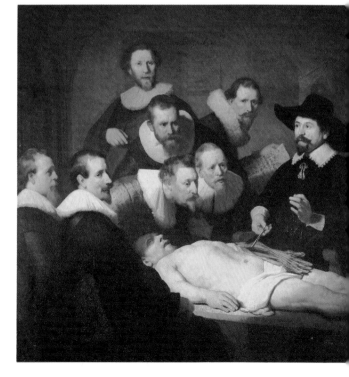

For his part, Alessandro made no secret of his disapproval. Despite this, Maria enrolled in medical school, although she agreed to her father's demand that she be accompanied on her walk to and from the school each day. She also agreed to sit apart from male students at lectures. These little rules didn't bother her too much.

Nor did she resent the practical problems, such as the lack of bathrooms for females at the school. What angered Maria much more was the attitude of her male fellow students. They would hiss and make rude remarks as she passed them in the corridors. These men would shake her desk when she was writing. They would laugh and interrupt if she asked the professors a question. They would shut her out of their discussions about the lectures.

There was nothing she could do at the time except swallow her anger. But later in her life, she always remembered how the male students had treated her. It was unfortunate, for her experiences at medical school were to shape her attitude toward men for the rest of her life.

Skeletons at night

A vital part of medical training is the examination and dissection of human bodies and organs, and the study of the skeleton and bone structure. According to the propriety of the time, the staff of the medical school could not agree to let Maria do this part of the course alongside male students. The answer they suggested was that she should do her laboratory work on her own in the evenings, after everyone had gone home.

Maria must have wondered, at times, if she had made the right choice of career. Working alone in the laboratories at night — among the skulls and skeletons and human organs in jars — she sometimes imagined that the skeletons were moving. She could not help thinking about the cruel ways the bodies she found herself working on — those of murderers or their victims — had met their deaths. She could tell herself — and she often did — not to be so silly; skeletons and dead human organs couldn't hurt her.

But there was something worse, something more threatening to her chosen career as a doctor. Maria

"A girl in Italy is too generally looked upon as the most brittle piece of china, which the least touch can crack."
A. Gallenga, in
Italy, Present and Future

"There, on the other side, the skeleton — ever more enormous — seemed to move. 'My God, what have I done to suffer in this way? Why me all alone in the midst of all this death?' ... A shiver ran through my bones."
Maria Montessori,
in a letter, 1896

found that the smell of the laboratories upset her and that she hated touching dead human tissue. What use, she wondered, would she be as a doctor?

One evening, working alone in the laboratory, she glanced out of the window and saw a young shop assistant of her own age going home from work. "She was outside, she was free, everything was alive around her," Maria thought. That was how a young woman should live, not surrounded by death. That night, Maria arrived home feeling sick. Her parents urged her to give up the course. It was not worth making herself ill. Maria went to bed in a fever. She could not sleep. At last, after tossing and turning for hours, she decided to write to her professor in the morning saying that she could not carry on.

It would have been a confession of failure to have written that letter. But the letter was never written. In the morning things didn't seem quite as bad as they

Lectures in chemistry were part of the course at medical school. As was the custom of the day, Maria sat apart from the men at such lectures. This in itself did not worry her — but it made access to the lecturer more difficult, especially as the male students would interrupt her if she asked a question.

16

had the previous night. Maria went to her lectures as usual and carried on with her studies.

The rights of women

Maria was still living at home and took great delight in embroidery, in dressing attractively, and in putting her hair up to show it at its best. She would always enjoy these gentler kinds of pleasures in her life.

But during this period she began to develop a deep lifelong commitment to the rights of women. From now on, she would campaign and work for the right of women to make their own career choices and not to depend on marriage for a fulfilling life.

There was a growing number of feminists across the world at this time. But one of the reasons for Maria's success in her campaign was her gentle and reasoned approach. "I have lived," she would later

"The woman of the future will have equal rights as well as equal duties. . . . Family life as we know it may change, but it is absurd to think that feminism will destroy motherly feelings. The new woman will marry and have children out of choice, not because marriage and motherhood are forced upon her."
Maria Montessori, speaking on "The New Woman," in 1899

A medical conference in Italy in 1905. By this time, Maria was in her second year as a lecturer in science and medicine at the University of Rome, but she was a lone figure. As this picture suggests, academic medicine was a world dominated by elderly men. For a woman to participate in it, except as a nurse, was thought revolutionary.

Fashionable wear for feminists when Maria was young included bloomers, baggy pantaloons named after Amelia Bloomer, who was among the first to adopt this style of dress. As a student, Maria became interested in the feminist movement, which was spreading across Europe and the United States. As a feminist, she preferred reasoned argument to confrontation as a way to gain rights for women.

tell a newspaper reporter, "a good deal among men, and observed the way they relate to women, and I think our aim should be to befriend them, not to alienate them from us."

Dr. Montessori

In 1896, after six grueling years, twenty-six-year-old Maria became the first woman in Italy to earn a degree in medicine. That same year she made her first journey outside Italy. She was chosen to speak at a feminist conference in Berlin on a subject very close to her heart — why women should be given the same pay as men for doing the same work. At that time, women in factories and on farms were paid considerably less than men.

Dr. Montessori had no fear of the audience. She stood up to give her first public speech without notes. Maria's speech was widely reported and, for the first time in her life, she knew what it was to be famous. Reporters wanted to interview her and photographers arrived to take her picture for the papers.

She returned from Berlin with a pile of enthusiastic press clippings. "What a lovely emancipated woman!" one journalist had written. "It seemed that everyone wanted to embrace her." Another wrote, "Her grace conquered all the pens — we might say all the hearts — of the journalists."

As a serious professional woman at the start of her career, with a strong interest in feminist issues, Maria Montessori had doubts about all these words about her appearance. It was what she had *said* and what she planned to *say* and *do* that she wanted reported. She wrote to her parents that on her return from Berlin, she would put her success there behind her and devote herself to serious work.

But she had recognized some talents in herself that would bring success throughout her life. She learned that she was able to make people notice her. She knew how to talk to the press. And she discovered that she enjoyed being in the limelight.

A talent for public speaking

In Berlin, Maria displayed a strong talent for public speaking. Her vibrant way of delivering her thoughts

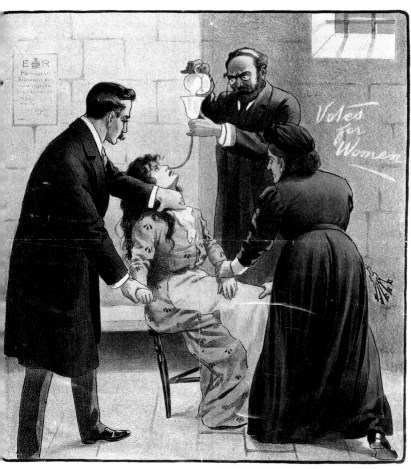

One aspect of feminism was the "Votes for Women" movement. Some protesters who were arrested went on a hunger strike when they reached prison and were forcibly fed.

and opinions captured her audience. It was, in fact, to do so every time she was to talk in public. Her expressive Italian voice was enhanced by her intensely animated gestures. These captivated audiences the world over.

To be able to speak in public can be learned or it can be a natural ability. For Maria Montessori, it was a natural gift and was part of the powerful charismatic allure that surrounded her. Her audiences would laugh along with her and clap at the right times. And she would cleverly guide them through the main points of her lecture.

She had had no previous experience. As the only

"She was a most attractive lecturer; her language so simple, so clear . . . that even the poorer students could understand her. All that she said had the warmth of life. I remember some students saying, 'Her lectures make us want to be good.'"
Anna Maria Maccheroni,
describing Maria's
1904-08 lectures
at the University of Rome

woman in medical school she had had no opportunity to even converse or debate with the male students. Most of her contributions were on paper — taken from experiments that she had undertaken in the evenings. She was not included as an equal in the everyday class discussions.

But she never lacked confidence. It was part of her character that any fears and doubts she might have had about her ability were kept inside herself.

Nor was she afraid of the outside world. She did not worry about what other people might think of her. This freedom from concern had shown up at medical school — it was not the taunts of the male students that upset her and resulted in her leaving medical school, but her own fear of whether she could cope with the scenes and smells in the laboratory.

The forgotten children

Maria's career blossomed. She became involved with adults and children, some who were perhaps mentally retarded and some who were thought to be. These children were often placed in institutions, sometimes with adults who were mentally retarded.

They were given no lessons and no toys to play with. Their lives were without excitement, completely empty. Children who were mentally retarded were written off as useless nuisances who were not worth any trouble or care.

Maria's interest in people with mental retardation led her to discover the work of two Frenchmen, Jean Itard and Edouard Seguin. In the first half of the nineteenth century, in Paris, these two men had specialized in educating both these children and children who were deaf.

They had refused to believe that people with mental retardation could not be educated, and by giving these people activities which exercised the senses of sight and touch, Itard and Seguin had made some progress.

Maria studied their work. She also read the books of Friedrich Froebel, a German who had founded schools for children up to seven years of age. As a result of this study, Maria realized a number of things.

First, it was possible to develop the ideas of Itard

Maria's first work was with people who had disabilities and were locked up in institutions. People with various disabilities were, at that time, locked away from the world and received minimal care. There was no attempt to train or educate them. Maria's experience in working with them convinced her that they could be given happier and more positive lives.

and Seguin further to help with the education of children who were mentally retarded. Second, this would be done better in special schools instead of in mental hospitals. Third, she needed to know more about education.

Commitment

Maria's energy was astonishing. Her full-time job was as an assistant doctor in a clinic for mentally ill patients. She was doing her own research work while she was practicing medicine.

She also ran a private medical clinic of her own, where she saw mainly women and children. On top of all this, she found time to be active in the newly formed National League for the Education of Retarded Children and to lecture on this subject and on feminism.

In 1899, when she was twenty-nine, Maria was asked to become director of a new school for mentally retarded children in Rome. She held this post for two years. She had been offered the job after giving a series of lectures in Rome on the education of these children. She was asked to give more lectures, and her lecture tours took her to London and Paris as well as to cities all over Italy.

These lectures attracted large audiences and huge coverage in the press. Some of this coverage, like the reports of the Berlin conference in 1896, concentrated more on the appearance and personality of "the beautiful scholar" than on what she had to say. But it also drew more attention to her two interests, feminism and the education of children.

In 1898 travel was far more of an adventure than it is today. For a young woman to travel on her own — and then to give a speech to a packed audience at the end of her journey — was almost unknown. But Maria Montessori was already setting a pattern that she was to follow to the end of her life. She was always ready to visit new places, meet new people, and find out what was happening in the world.

A woman's place

In her feminist lectures on "The New Woman," Maria attacked the prejudices of male academics,

"I speak for the six million Italian women who work in factories and on farms as long as eighteen hours a day for pay that is often half of what men earn for the same work and sometimes even less."

Maria Montessori, at the Berlin Women's Congress, 1896

When working with children who were disabled, Maria didn't know it was to lead to her life's work. Most doctors just gave physical care. Not Maria. Her sensitivity and commitment compelled her to provide more for children.

Opposite, left: After she left medical school, Maria found time in her busy life to run a free clinic for poor women and children. This is the background to the best-known photograph of her as a young woman: She had given free treatment to a poor dressmaker, who made her this lace dress as a present. It was not Maria's style, but she arranged for a photograph to be taken of her wearing it and presented the picture to the dressmaker. It was taken in 1898.

particularly scientists, at a time when "experts" produced all kinds of unproven theories to explain what they called the "inferiority" of women.

For example, one distinguished scientist declared that the brain of a woman contained less phosphorus than the brain of a man, and this held back a woman's intelligence. When Maria would mention such examples as these in her lectures, she managed to produce many laughs — she was entertaining as well as insightful.

The answer, Maria said, was for women to educate themselves in science so that they could argue against prejudices "with their brains, not just their hearts." She looked forward to a future when women would be confident enough to make sure that they got what they wanted — equal pay, peace in the world, freedom to have children or not as they chose.

In this argument, she was well ahead of her time. It is only in the second half of this century, long after her death, that women have begun to win the fight for equality and against prejudice.

Mario Montessori

Maria Montessori's life was not all work. One of her colleagues at the school for mentally retarded children was a fellow doctor, Giuseppe Montesano. The two fell in love. Maria never spoke in public about this. Only her family and very closest friends knew anything about it, so no one else knows for certain why the relationship failed.

We do know, however, that at some time between 1898 and 1901, Maria had a son, Mario, whose father was Dr. Montesano. (Mario himself dates his birth as March 31, 1898.) At that time, in Italy, it was a matter of shame for a woman, especially a professional woman, to have a baby outside marriage. So this could have caused serious problems for Maria. She, like other women in this circumstance, would have to find ways to support herself and her child if she were not married to the baby's father.

For some reason, Giuseppe Montesano failed to marry her and later married someone else. The birth of Mario was kept a close secret by the Montessori family and their friends. As a baby, he was sent to live

*Above: There was no
shortage of poor patients
for Maria's clinic. The
streets of Rome were full of
poor families like this,
badly housed, under-
nourished, and vulnerable
to any disease that passed
by. The fathers of these
families had no regular
work, but depended on
what work they could pick
up from day to day.*

with a family in the country. Brought up as one of their children, he was a teenager before he knew who his real mother was.

A student again

The birth of her baby brought about a crisis in Maria's life — she had been let down by Giuseppe Montesano. Several times in her life, when she was faced with problems, Maria Montessori sought to forget them by burying herself in a new work project. It happened at medical school.

Now it happened again. Perhaps because of the birth of her child and then the loss of him, she began to take a greater interest in matters affecting the lives of children.

She decided to give up her post as director of the school in Rome and to return to the university as a student of teaching methods, hygiene, and psychology. It began to look as if Maria Montessori was steadily moving toward the one career that she had insisted she was not interested in: teaching.

When Maria became directly involved in education, she was determined to produce an atmosphere different from the one prevailing at the time. This contemporary group photograph of an Italian girls' school sums up what she was rebelling against: unsmiling formality and rigid rules.

The training of teachers then, as it does now, included periods of observation and practical teaching in schools. With the experience of her two years as director of the Rome school for mentally retarded children behind her, Maria was horrified by what she saw in schools for children of normal intelligence.

They were still places where children were told to sit up straight in rows. They were placed into overly large classes. They merely chanted back the words of their teachers. Dull methods of teaching made the children lose whatever interest in lessons — or in the world — they might have had. Children who should have done well at school were doing badly because they were so poorly taught.

Maria likened the atmosphere in schools to prisons. The teachers spoke harshly, rarely smiled, appeared to dislike children, and gave punishments for the slightest reasons. The buildings were drab and gloomy. It was no wonder that children behaved badly and avoided going to school if they could.

Children love to learn

As she studied, Maria Montessori became more and more convinced that the methods she had used with pupils who were mentally retarded *could* be adapted for children of normal intelligence. She went on to develop many ideas about children, and these ideas are now accepted without question.

For one thing, she related the ability of children to learn to their physical health and diet. She also pioneered the idea that forcing children to learn was wrong. Children *wanted* to learn, she would insist. If they were given the right materials and challenging learning experiences, they would do so.

Maria's research proved to her that children went through a period of sensitivity between the ages of two and a half and six years. During this time, their minds were open to learning in a different way than they were during any other age.

The materials Montessori developed and the environment she created for the children gave them the opportunities to try out their independence and to use their newly emerging reasoning powers, even at that young age.

"On one occasion I had tried a child with nearly all the objects of the series without exciting the smallest spark of interest; then I casually showed him the two tablets of red and blue colors, and called his attention to the difference of tint. He seized them at once with a kind of thirstiness and learnt five different colors in a single lesson."

The headmistress of the
first Montessori school
in the United States

Back on course

By 1904 Maria, now thirty-four, seemed to have bounced back from her life crisis. She was lecturing and writing articles for magazines as well as papers on medical and educational topics.

During that year she was put in charge of a training course for teachers at the University of Rome. "She was," wrote a student who attended at the time, "a most attractive lecturer with a manner that was easy and gracious." Education courses were believed to be dull. But Montessori had the ability to make the study of this important field fascinating and inspiring for her students.

Trainee teachers flocked to her lectures and came away excited by what they had heard. They had been looking forward without much pleasure to a career of teaching children as if these children were parrots. Maria Montessori inspired them to have a more interesting vision of what teaching could be. Many of

A caricature of the nineteenth-century view of children in school: if the teacher's back was turned, the children would behave badly. The message was that children were little savages who had to be tamed, by physical punishment if necessary.

An English "dame school" in the nineteenth century. These were schools for poor children whose parents paid a penny to the teacher each week. The emphasis was on keeping still. "It is very clear," wrote Maria Montessori, "that since the adult has had no notion of how important activity is to the child, he has simply prevented such disturbing activity."

the students who attended her lectures in Rome were later to join her as teachers at her Children's House.

As for Maria, she was about to start on her life's work. Her starting point was the Casa dei Bambini in San Lorenzo.

The core of the Montessori Method is the belief that children want to work and will do so conscientiously provided that the work is appropriate to their age and development. These letter cards form part of the Montessori materials. Before learning to read and write, the child traces the letter forms, which are in sandpaper on a glossy background, and so commits them to memory through the sense of touch.

Discovering the senses

The equipment Maria developed is central to her method and is vital to the learning process. The "sensory materials" were designed to give children a variety of experiences through the senses — touch, sight, hearing, or smell. She even touched on their sense of the weight of objects.

There were sets of straight-sided cylinders of different diameters and a board with holes into which the cylinders fit exactly. There were wooden cubes in sizes ranging from one centimeter to ten centimeters. These could be used to build a tower.

There were prism-shaped rods, square rods, boards, and cards with surfaces of differing roughness, various kinds of woven materials, and trays with different geometric shapes to be fitted into them. Each set of materials taught a different concept, such as measurement, counting, or volume. Using sensory material, even four-year-old children were able to teach themselves mathematical and geometrical concepts that had usually been taught only to teenage pupils.

The children were allowed to experiment with the materials, once they had been shown how to use them, often learning this from each other. At San Lorenzo, Candida Nuccitelli supervised the children, answering questions and taking care of them. When she could spare the time, Maria Montessori spent a morning or afternoon at the Children's House making notes on the children's development.

From her observations of these children, Maria began to work out what she would later call the Montessori Method. The idea behind the method was that it grew out of what children did naturally. Maria believed that children knew how to teach themselves.

And even in schools that do not follow all of Montessori's ideas, this particular one — the idea that education begins with the child, not the teacher — has become one of the keystones in the education of young children. Later, Dr. Montessori wrote up her observations at the Children's House and showed how they had led her to important new pieces of knowledge about how children behave and learn.

She described how one little girl of three had been working with the cylinders and the board into which they fitted. Maria watched the girl do the same exercise over and over again with such concentration that she took no notice of anything else that was happening in the room. When she had fitted the cylinders into the holes forty-two times, she suddenly "stopped, as though coming out of a dream, and smiled as if she were very happy. Her eyes shone."

Maria wondered why the girl had wanted to repeat the same exercise so many times, and why, after the forty-second time, she felt that her task was finished. It was, she wrote, "a first glimpse into the unexplored depths of the child's mind."

"The children seemed to begin to find their own way; in many of the objects they had first despised as silly playthings, they began to discover a novel interest, and as a result of this new interest, they began to act as independent individuals."
The headmistress of the first Montessori school in the United States

"The Montessori material does not enter the child's life as a hard and forbidding task to be accomplished; but rather as a door through which each child enters a fuller life."
Dr. Helen Helming, head of a German Montessori training college

This glimpse led her to believe that children needed to repeat exercises that they have done before. Perhaps it gave them a feeling of security before they tried something new.

It began to emerge quite clearly — and is visible in any Montessori school today — that the children had a great need for order and tidiness. Each child would use a particular object or set of materials and very neatly put it back in its place on the shelf again.

This gave every child in the "house" the security of knowing that any object, provided it was not already being used by someone, would always be in its proper place ready for use. It also gave each child a respect for the materials themselves and for the other children using them.

Freedom of choice

Maria learned another important lesson one day from a story that Candida told her. Candida had arrived late one morning, and the children were already in the

A novel feature of the Montessori approach was that children should be encouraged to learn outdoors. Educators of the time feared that children out of the classroom would run riot, especially when no teacher was in sight. Not so, Maria argued, if absorbing and purposeful activities were provided.

room. The cupboard where the sensory materials were kept had been left unlocked, and the children had already been to it and taken out some of the materials to work with.

Candida was angry.

The children were thieves, she said, and needed to be punished.

Maria did not agree.

The children, she said, had shown that they were keen to start work and that they knew what to do. They did not need the help of an adult to get started and, more important, had made their own choice of which materials to take out of the cupboard. Instead of being punished, they should be praised.

More observations followed from this incident. Maria was interested to find that among all the materials she had provided, some were in great demand while others were ignored.

She thought that this was perhaps because the children did not understand how to use the items that

"I cannot tell you what a joy it has been to me to read your book. I have always felt that children should be treated as you treat them . . . and that they should be allowed to do things for themselves. Everyone told me I was mad because I was always hoping a new kind of school would be born, and now I know that I was right."

A Chinese teacher, in a letter to Maria, 1909

Maria Montessori believed that young children should be given real activities to carry out, not make-believe ones. Another of her beliefs was that children should be given responsibility for their environment. In Montessori schools, domestic tasks such as preparing food, and real outdoor activities such as planting, weeding, and watering, play an important part.

they were ignoring, so she decided to show the children what could be done with them.

Still they remained unused and gathering dust. This taught her that it was for the children to choose what they wanted to do, not for the teacher to interfere. The children must have freedom of choice and independence.

Children want to work

In this way, Maria gradually built up her picture of the way children learn. It fascinated her to try to see inside a child's mind, especially if the child did something unexpected.

One thing that particularly interested her was that although there were plenty of toys in the Casa, the children preferred to work with the sensory materials. It became clear that the children preferred work to play. They wanted to learn, but they wanted to learn in the way they themselves chose.

Adults would feel the same, Maria said, if they were forced to play cards or chess all the time.

Maria found that at the Casa dei Bambini, the children quickly came to enjoy themselves. There they were not made to do things they didn't want to do and were not shouted at or punished. The children had not been given any medical treatment, yet they had a healthy look about them that had been missing from their pale, underfed faces. The sullen and crying children of that first day became happy, friendly, clean, orderly, and involved in what they were doing.

As money allowed, more activities were introduced. The children helped to prepare and serve their lunch. Flowers and plants were brought along and were kept watered by the children. There were pets to look after. In fact, slowly the room at San Lorenzo came to look very similar to any nursery school or kindergarten today.

More Children's Houses

The first Casa was so successful that within a few months Maria was asked to open a second, in another apartment block in San Lorenzo. Meanwhile, richer parents from other parts of Rome were offering to pay her to set up a Casa for their children.

There were distinguished visitors to the Children's Houses. There were newspaper and magazine articles. In 1908 a third Casa opened in Milan, and in 1909 a fourth opened, again in Rome.

By 1909, Maria's work had stopped being a series of experiments in education by a single doctor. It became a movement.

Among the people who backed her were an Italian nobleman, Baron Leopoldo Franchetti, and his American wife. They were rich landowners who had become interested in improving the lives of the people who lived on their land.

One of the ways the Franchettis wanted to do this was by providing schools and as a result, they had visited the Children's House. The Franchettis and Maria became friends, and she was invited to spend the summer of 1909 with them at their villa near Citta di Castello high in the Apennine Mountains.

Maria's first book

While she was there, Montessori gave a series of lectures to about a hundred students and other interested people. It was to be the first training course in the Montessori Method.

When it was completed, the Franchettis persuaded Maria to write a book based on her lectures. She titled her book *The Montessori Method* and published it in Italy in 1910. It was later to be translated into more than twenty languages.

Although Maria wrote a modern version later, this version contained all the basic ideas of her approach to educating young children.

In the book, she describes how she had come to understand what children wanted and needed by watching them closely at work at the Children's Houses. They enjoyed repeating the same actions, like the girl with the cylinders.

They liked having freedom of choice, like the children who had found the cupboard open. They liked things in order, as they showed when they put things away at the day's end. Children did not learn anything useful through rewards or punishments. They had a natural sense of dignity; it was important to them that they be clean and well behaved.

"Education is a natural process spontaneously carried out by the human individual and is acquired not by listening to words but by experiences in the environment."
Maria Montessori

"Montessori . . . makes it her aim to create round the child a real and sensible world; and to do it in such a way that the child can act and work in this world independently of the adult . . . carrying out real activities with real responsibilities. In short the child will be able to take a part in the world just as . . . seriously as the grown-up."
Professor K. Gerhards, in An Assessment of Montessori Teaching, 1928

Tall stories?

Some of Maria's "discoveries" seemed to be the opposite of what was generally believed about children. She even claimed that the children at the Casa dei Bambini refused to eat sweets because they thought they were unnatural and unnecessary. Naturally, the general reaction to this "discovery" was one of disbelief. After all, everyone knew that children loved candies, cakes, cookies, and other sweets. The popular idea was that they would eat all they could.

And as for children naturally liking things to be in order, adults thought that was nonsense too. They believed that children loved to make a mess and that they soon got bored and began to fidget.

Maria's approach to education was open to a lot of criticism but her answer was that she hadn't dreamed up her ideas out of thin air. They all arose out of her close observation of the children themselves and out of the questions she had asked herself about why they behaved as they did. Often, she had not believed her

The Montessori Method places great emphasis on precise, ordered movement. These children in a London Montessori school are carefully following a line chalked on the floor. Some of Maria Montessori's critics said that activities like this were too restrictive. Her reply was that they were essential exercises in "the language of movement."

34

own eyes and repeated experiments over and over again to check her observations.

Take the refusal of sweets, for example: "This seemed to me so extraordinary that I wished to repeat the test again and again, for everyone knows that children are always greedy for sweets. I took sweets to school, but the children refused them or put them in the pockets of their aprons.

"Thinking that since they were poor they wanted to take the sweets home to their families, I told them, 'These sweets are for you, and here are others for you to take home.' They took them, but they put them all in their pockets and did not eat them."

Maria herself could find no explanation for this except that perhaps eating sweets took the children's minds off other things they would rather be doing. But if anyone she told this story to doubted it, she would take them into the Children's House, offer the children sweets, and prove she was telling the truth.

The love of silence

Another discovery of Maria's caused people to ask for proof. Children, she claimed, had a great love for silence. Her critics could hardly believe this! Passing by a children's playground would be enough proof to show how much noise children make. But again, Maria had a story and proof to back up her theory.

One day she brought into the Children's House a sleeping four-month-old baby. She drew the children's attention to how quiet it was and suggested that none of them could keep as still and quiet as that. They all tried, and soon the room was absolutely quiet. No one moved. All that could be heard was the ticking of the clock, a drop of water dripping somewhere, the buzzing of flies.

Writing about this experience later, Maria said that the children were not keeping quiet and still just because she had asked them to. They stayed quiet because they were actually *enjoying* the silence.

The experience led Maria to work out something she called the "Silence Game" which was played in the Children's Houses. It began while the children were working; the teacher would put up a notice with just one simple word — *Silence* — written on it.

"It took time for me to convince myself that all this was not an illusion. After each new experience proving such a truth I said to myself, 'I won't believe it yet. I'll believe in it next time.'"

Maria Montessori, in
The Secret of Childhood

"As each child in turn notices it, at once pencils, chalks, letters, rods, counters, beads or whatever it is they are working with are quietly put down. . . . Before long all the little hands have ceased to work, and all the little bodies have become motionless. A calm has spread over the room, as over a pond when the wind has dropped."

The teacher now drew the curtains and walked silently to the door. She opened it quietly and glided out without a sound, leaving the door open behind her.

"For a while nothing happens, except . . . the 'sounds of silence' which come stealing out 'like mice' — the creaking of a chair, the ticking of a clock, a distant train, the twitter of birds in the garden, a door banging in a remote corridor, far-off strains of music.

"Through the semi-darkness she sees a child rising to his feet. Very slowly and very cautiously he lifts his little chair and . . . replaces it on the floor without a sound. Now . . . he begins to thread his way in and out amongst the little tables until he vanishes through the open door. Then another child rises. . . . Then another, and another. And so, one by one, they all rise and disappear."

Mystery

Maria used to love to demonstrate the Silence Game to visitors. The question they always asked afterward was why the children had left the room one at a time, and how a particular child knew when to go. The answer was that once outside the door, the teacher would very softly — in "the ghost of a whisper" — say the names one by one.

For Maria, this was more than just a game. She believed it demonstrated how much young children enjoy silence and will make a great deal of effort to preserve it. She believed that children's liking for silence went back to before they were born and brought suddenly from the silence of the womb into a world of noise and bustle.

Some people who criticized the Montessori Method later said that the Silence Game was simply a matter of training children to do what the teacher wanted. Certainly it could look like that, a kind of teacher's "party trick," yet Maria could point to the

"The first essential for a child's development is concentration. They must find out how to concentrate and for this they need things to concentrate upon."
Maria Montessori, in The Montessori Method

experiences of children's responses in her schools that had led her to try the Silence Game. As she always said, the child came first.

The very essence of Maria's teaching and her personality was to give children a chance to be calm, peaceful, and organized within themselves. Her own persona was surrounded by a sense of calm and control which always drew people to her. The Montessori students began to develop their own sense of peace through using the materials in the Children's House in the Montessori way. Her aim was to give the children a chance to be at one with themselves and, therefore, to bring about a more peace-loving and calm generation for the future.

There was nothing in *The Montessori Method* that was not based on what she had seen and tried for herself. And, as with the children who refused sweets, there was no point in telling the story of the Silence Game unless it was true.

"The cat sat on the mat"

Most people would say that learning to read and write is the most important thing that happens in a child's first years of school. But at first, Maria was more interested in helping children to "discover themselves" and to investigate the world around them than she was in teaching them skills. She found, however, that mothers who brought their children to her *expected* her to teach reading and writing, so she set about finding a method.

Learning to read and write in ordinary schools in those days was a grim business. Children learned sentences by heart from wall posters or from books. They often earned a rap on the knuckles with a ruler if they hesitated or got a word wrong. Endlessly, they recited sentences like "The cat sat on the mat."

They copied out letters in chalk on slates and, later, into "copybooks." These books had page after page of writing exercises. It was not surprising that even after years of this dull routine, many children failed to learn to read and write. They were not motivated. That is, no one suggested to them that reading and writing could give them pleasure and entertainment.

"Listening to silence" is another Montessori exercise. "Silence," Maria wrote, "often brings us the knowledge which we had not fully realized, that we possess within ourselves an inner life." But unlike conventional teachers, who enforced quiet with the cane, Maria turned silence into a game and used it to reveal to children a lost world of quiet sound.

The "writing explosion"

Following her previous experience, Maria Montessori felt that children would learn to read and write if they themselves really wanted to. As with all learning, she felt it should be pleasurable. It should be fun.

Once again, Maria turned the traditional rules of teaching upside-down. It was usual to teach reading first. Maria started her children with writing. Watching the children working with her sensory materials, she had seen how sensitive they were to different degrees of roughness and smoothness. She built on this to teach them the letters of the alphabet.

She cut out the letter shapes in sandpaper, glued them onto pieces of smooth cardboard, and encouraged the children to trace the sandpaper shapes

Maria Montessori believed that children were particularly susceptible to learning certain skills at specific ages, which she called "sensitive periods." One of these was at age four, when — she said — children could learn simple number facts if presented with appropriate materials. Certainly this four-year-old seems to be enjoying learning numbers!

with their fingers. These gave the children a feel of the letter — its shape and its curves and straight lines — so that it became real to the senses. The children then had a physical knowledge of the letter and could move on to actually writing and forming the letter much more quickly and easily.

The very delicate and precise differences between the textures of materials enabled the children to refine their understanding and to give them an increased sensitivity to the world around them.

Their minds became open to much more than reading and writing; they were open to the whole spectrum of senses. This method proved a great success. The children moved from tracing the shapes to writing them for themselves. There was, as Maria wrote later, an explosion of interest in writing. "They wrote everywhere — on doors, on walls, and even at home on loaves of bread."

Reading

It was after the children could write that they began to move on to reading. Here, Maria initially made a mistake. Once they could read the words they had written, she thought the children would be ready for books. But when she handed some books around, they took no interest in them.

Instead, they started reading anything they could find in the classroom, such as messages on the board or the words on a notice that had been pinned up.

"At the same time," Maria reported, "their parents came to tell us that in the street the children would stop to read shop signs, so that it was impossible to go out for walks with them."

It was only after weeks of this that the children came to take an interest in reading from books. It was as if this kind of reading was less important than reading things in the "real" world. Maria wrote later about how an interest in books finally came:

"A child came to school full of excitement, hiding in his hand a crumpled piece of paper. . . .

'Guess what's in this piece of paper.'

'There's nothing. It's just a torn piece of paper.'

'No, there's a story.'

"The child had picked up the paper from a rubbish

"They took the geometrical insets, the graduated cylinders and began to touch the outlines of the wooden forms with their fingers; the younger children showed a preference for the buttoning and lacing frames; they took one after the other without any signs of fatigue and seemed delighted with the new objects. An atmosphere of industry pervaded the schoolroom."
An early Montessori teacher in England

heap," Maria went on, "and he began to read the story. Then at last they grasped the significance of books, and after this the books went like hot cakes."

Materials fit for a child

The sets of boards with letters made of sandpaper glued onto them were to become basic Montessori equipment for the first stages of teaching children to write and, later, to read. They are still used in Montessori schools today. Meanwhile, Maria was trying out learning materials for arithmetic and other more advanced subjects.

Devising new materials took up a great deal of time. It was not simply a matter of having an idea and finding someone to make the sets of materials. Maria would take an experimental set along to the Casa and try it out with the children. Sometimes she would find, as she did at first with books, that she was starting something before the children were ready for it. Sometimes the materials would be difficult for the children to handle. Everything that became part of the Montessori Method was patiently tried and tried again until it was exactly right.

All the materials were bright and shiny and geometrically shaped, and all were designed for child-sized hands.

The quality of the blocks, bells, counting beads, cylinders, and rods meant that they lasted even after constant use by the children. They allowed the children to make their own discoveries about the material they chose.

For example, to grasp slight differences in tone, the children and the teacher used rows of bells on alternate black and white strips of wood. One set of bells had a label with the name of its note written on it while one set was blank; on hearing the two bells, the child could match the two together.

The care and patience they needed to bring to this task in order to get it right gave the children a satisfying sense of achievement.

Popularity

At the same time, Maria was in increasing demand as a lecturer and as a consultant in setting up new

Beads as a means of teaching numbers to young children are now common in schools, but Maria Montessori was a pioneer of this method.

Opposite: A selection of modern Montessori materials. From the beginning, Maria insisted that her materials should be bright, of good quality, and easy for children to hold and use. The materials used in Montessori schools today are copies of those that Maria developed after trial and error in the first of her Children's Houses.

40

In 1919, Maria went to England to give the first of her training courses there. She was received enthusiastically, as she was all over the world. Four years later, the University of Durham conferred on her an honorary doctorate of letters. She is seen here in the academic robes she wore for the ceremony.

Children's Houses. The call for more Children's Houses meant that more Montessori-trained people would be needed to run them. Where was Maria to find the time to do all this, or how would she find the help she needed?

She came to another important decision. She was still a lecturer in science and education at the University of Rome, as well as at a women's college. Moreover, she still had a private medical practice. Maria decided to give up all this work and concentrate her energies on her own method and movement.

It was a decision that took a good deal of courage. Maria needed to earn enough money to support herself. Her university lecturing and her clinic had provided her with a good living. If she gave these up, would her fees for lecturing on her method, writing books, and setting up new Children's Houses be enough to live on?

Into the unknown

Maria decided to take the risk. She was now so interested in the education of young children that she did not want to spend time on other things. Although some years later she had a period of money worries, she managed for the rest of her life to make her method provide her with a living.

In Italy, she was helped from the start by a group of wealthy people who formed a Montessori Society to support her work. The students from Maria's training courses would eventually settle throughout Europe and then in Britain and the United States.

Soon, Montessori societies were founded in these countries as well. By 1911, four years after the first Casa was opened, the Montessori Method had become the approved teaching system in state schools in Italy and Switzerland.

Montessori schools were being planned in India, China, Mexico, Korea, Argentina, and Hawaii. The tsar of Russia had even opened a Montessori school in his palace in St. Petersburg for his own five children and the children of his courtiers.

Rich and poor parents alike wanted their young children to learn the Montessori way. The Montessori movement had become worldwide.

The news spreads

At the beginning of the twentieth century, there was no radio and no television, so news spread slowly.

This makes it all the more surprising that the news of what Maria Montessori was doing in her Children's Houses went around the world so quickly.

In 1910, only three years after Maria opened her first Casa dei Bambini, the owner of *McClure's Magazine*, a leading American magazine, heard about her work and asked a journalist to write an article about it. The nineteen-page article, with photographs of Maria Montessori, the Children's Houses, and her materials, was printed in the May 1911 issue.

The editor was enthusiastic about the article. But no one had given so much space to pieces on education in popular magazines. He was delighted when, after the magazine came out, he had to go back to the printers for extra copies. And he was amazed when sacks full of letters from readers began to arrive at his office.

American readers wanted to know more about the Montessori Method. They wanted to know how they could join one of Maria's training courses. They wanted to know how they could use her ideas in their own schools.

By the end of 1911, the first Montessori school in the United States had been opened in New York. It was run by an American teacher who had been trained by Maria in Rome. This school would be the first of many in the United States.

By 1913 there were over a hundred Montessori schools in the United States — or rather, there were over a hundred schools that claimed to follow the Montessori Method.

Not all were directed by people who had attended one of Maria's courses in Rome. This was unfortunate, for Maria believed that only teachers trained by her were qualified to use her method.

But she learned that there were teachers in the United States who were setting up "Montessori" schools after a quick reading of her books or of books about her.

Many of these schools had very little in common with the Children's Houses. They might have been

"If parents shall learn from Dr. Montessori something of the value of child life . . . and of its possibilities, and apply this knowledge widely, the work of the great Italian educator will be successful enough."
Professor Henry W. Holmes
of Harvard University, 1912

The set of "cylinders" of varying diameters and, later, of varying heights was among the materials that Maria devised for children aged from two and a half to three. Each cylinder has only one correct position in the block. Maria claimed that children, having "got it right," would repeat the exercise up to forty times without losing interest.

inspired by her theories, but they ignored whole aspects of Maria's carefully researched work.

This angered Maria, with good reason. These poorly run schools were giving her methods a bad reputation. One critic, having visited one such school, wrote that "the children are being petted and allowed to have their own way until they get an exalted idea of their importance."

This was far from the way things were in real Montessori schools. No one who had seen Maria in action in the schoolroom could believe that the children were allowed to have entirely their own way. Some of her critics even complained that she gave them too little freedom.

All kinds of people in the United States — owners of private schools, newspaper and magazine editors, book publishers, toy makers, even filmmakers — were starting to use the Montessori name. In November 1913, Maria set sail for New York in the hope of claiming her name back for herself.

Success in the United States

Maria was now forty-three. She was no longer "the beautiful scholar." She had put on weight, and her hair was beginning to look silvery. But she still had a great deal of physical stamina. She came through the battery of newspaper interviews and picture calls in New York with an inner calmness, as if she had been used to such attention all her life.

Her tour was demanding. She spoke in New York, Washington, Boston, Pittsburgh, and Chicago. In those days, public lectures by famous people were good business. People would pack the lecture halls in much the same way as, today, they would tune in to watch a television interview with someone famous.

Maria's tour was a huge success. Yet she still suspected that there were too many people in the United States using her name to make money for themselves. A few years later she was to find out how true this was.

In 1915 Montessori made her second visit to the United States and took part in a world exhibition being held in San Francisco. In the exposition's main hall, Maria arranged for a Casa to be built for visitors.

Above: Intense involvement in the activity at hand is characteristic of children in schools using the Montessori Method.

Left: The Montessori movement has grown worldwide. Maria's method is used in private and public schools, in churches, in village halls, and in remote villages. Conditions vary from place to place, but Maria's ideas and the materials she developed from them remain the core of this world movement.

Its walls were of glass, which allowed visitors to observe as demonstrations of the Montessori Method were going on inside. Visitors went away from San Francisco excited by what they had seen and wanting to find out more. Montessori was pleased to see that newspaper articles and pictures of the glass school rapidly found their way all over the world.

Farewell to America

In making Maria's name more widely known, the second visit was as hugely successful as the first. Her fame had spread worldwide — she was Italy's most famous person. But the interest she had aroused clarified the problems of one person trying to keep control of a worldwide movement. Maria had a full schedule of work in Italy which she would not hand over to others.

The sea voyage from Europe to the United States took six or seven days and, while World War I lasted, ships were open to attacks by German submarines. It was impossible for Maria to supervise the American Montessori movement from Rome, but it was also impossible for her to run it on the spot.

According to some sources, she refused to hand over the movement in the United States to someone else. Other sources say that when she left the United States, she left her program in charge of Helen Parkhurst, who later developed her own system of education called the Dalton Method.

Whatever is the case, the result was that the movement in the United States broke up in endless quarrels and bitterness. Companies making toys and educational games took up her ideas and used her name without permission.

Not everyone who wanted to teach by the Montessori Method could afford to travel to Rome to learn directly from her — yet she insisted that it was the only way. Teachers and others involved in the field of education who had wanted to use Maria's methods finally moved on to other interests. Maria never made any publicized trips to the United States again, visiting only for personal reasons, the last time in 1918. It was not until after her death that American interest in her approach to education revived.

The "prepared environment"

In 1914, Maria published her *Dr. Montessori's Own Handbook*. Her experience with the growing number of Children's Houses led her to describe what she regarded as the perfect room for young children to learn in. While today, the ideas suggested in the handbook can be seen in operation in Montessori schools and most other schools for young children, in 1914, they were new and exciting.

A Children's House, Montessori wrote, "ought to be a real house; that is to say, a set of rooms with a garden of which the children are the masters. A garden which contains shelters is ideal, because the children can play or sleep under them, and can also bring their tables out to work or dine. In this way they may live almost entirely in the open air, and are protected at the same time from rain and sun."

The furniture, Maria went on, should be painted brightly and be light enough for children to move. In addition to wooden chairs, there should be small wicker armchairs and sofas. An important feature of the main room is a long, low cupboard for the learning materials. This should be designed so that the smallest child can have access to it to choose his or her materials. The design of this cupboard went back to the San Lorenzo Casa and the tall cupboard which the children had raided when Candida Nuccitelli was late. This had demonstrated to Maria the importance of furniture low enough for the children to use safely.

The ideal room should also have blackboards fixed low enough on the walls for the children to use, and should be made pleasant with pictures, plants, and flowers. There should be rugs that the children could spread on the floor and sit on.

But the Montessori Method was not simply a matter of providing special learning materials and child-sized furniture. Maria Montessori was concerned with what happens in childhood. Her studies and observation of young children had led her to believe that childhood was a frightening place.

Fear began as soon as a baby was born. "The child," she wrote with understanding and sympathy, "has just come from a place where not the faintest ray of light, or the faintest sound, could reach. He arrives

Maria addressing the Panama-Pacific International Exposition in San Francisco in 1915. Although she spoke a number of languages fluently, she always gave her lectures in Italian. Even this did not hamper her — she seemed able to charm and convert any audience.

In a Montessori classroom, everything is to the child's scale. Nothing is out of reach. The children have free access to the materials and can return one set and choose another whenever they wish. The low cupboards and shelves are used because Maria discovered at the Casa dei Bambini that the children wanted to put away the materials themselves rather than let the teacher do it. This reflected, she said, the child's instinctive desire for order.

worn out by the immense contrast between absolute rest and the . . . effort of birth."

At once, Maria Montessori said, the baby emerges into a big, frightening, and confusing world. Things happen that the child does not expect. The baby has not had enough experience to expect anything and does not understand any of it. All the child knows is that she or he needs food, warmth, and love.

As children grow, Maria believed, more and more adults turn up to tell them what to do. Adults are all strong. Children are weak. Maria thought it was not surprising that so many children were shy or sullen or badly behaved. They needed to be able to decide for themselves what to do. They deserved to be able to make their own choices. Teachers, she came to insist, should "follow the child."

This was the thinking that lay behind the Montessori Method. It involved understanding the child's point of view. It meant studying children and figuring out the reasons for what they did. In that way, Maria believed, it was the children who taught the teachers, not the other way around.

Plenty of detail

In the early days of the Montessori movement, few people argued with Maria's methods because the results were there to see in the Children's Houses — busy rooms full of eager activity, with children learning at their own pace but in a way controlled by the materials they were given. But there were soon worries about the way in which Maria presented her method and controlled its use, and even about the method itself.

The Montessori Method and her other books contained a vast amount of sound advice and good sense that had been proved in practice. But it was wrapped in a view of childhood that many people thought to be too sentimental. Maria seemed to think of childhood almost as a state of holiness. The child, she seemed to say, was always right and the adult always wrong. Some readers, while seeing the good sense of her teaching methods, could not bring themselves to accept these views.

Maria also continuously made detailed lists of instructions, possibly as a result of her scientific training. In *The Montessori Method*, she even described the amount and type of food that a child should have each day. There should be one gram of meat to every cubic centimeter of gravy. Eggs should be eaten only when they are still warm from the nest. Children should not be given cheese or raw vegetables, and preferably no vegetables at all except spinach. And so on.

There was even a correct Montessori way, which she demonstrated in her lectures, to blow one's nose. Her goal in these demonstrations was to teach the children "personal dignity."

Maria's disciples

Although she was a witty and amusing lecturer, Maria seems to have been less lighthearted in her private life. She took criticism badly. She did not like it when her students questioned her ideas or argued with her. The result was that members of the Montessori

"Instead of being trained to be a member of the family the boy of today is taught to be President of the United States. The children are being petted and allowed to have their own way until they get an exalted idea of their importance."
A critic of a school that was passing itself off as a Montessori school but was not following the Montessori Method, quoted in The New York Times, 1913

"After the age of four, fillet of beef may be introduced into the diet, but never heavy and fat meats like that of the pig, the capon, the eel, the tuna, etc., which are to be absolutely excluded along with oysters and lobsters."
Maria Montessori, in The Montessori Method

Maria (holding a bouquet) in the middle of a group of students at a training course she held in London in 1929. Her following of admirers was enormous, but it tended to be exclusive. This led to disputes, especially in the United States, with those who approved of her methods but were not members of the charmed circle allowed to call her "Mammolina."

movement — those who stayed in her courses and went on to become Montessori teachers — were people who accepted without question everything she said and almost worshipped her.

This inner circle of admirers was allowed to call her *Mammolina*, "darling mamma." To everyone else she was *la Dottoressa*, "the lady doctor." She reinforced her position as the sole head of the movement by insisting that only people trained personally by her could be Montessori teachers. Only she was allowed to pass on her method to others.

This was not good for Maria, who would have benefited from knowing some people with personalities as strong as hers who could challenge her. Nor was it good for the Montessori movement, for while it grew in numbers it did not grow in ideas. All of its principles and practices were tied to the ideas of one woman.

In both Britain and the United States, quarrels

broke out between "Maria's disciples" — those who accepted her ideas without question — and other teachers who wanted to adapt the Montessori Method or add new ideas to it. This argument went on throughout the 1920s, as more people in the educational world came to see the value of Maria's work, and also to question some aspects of it.

Wasted energy

There are two sides to the argument. On the one hand Maria depended for her living on the movement she had created, on the sale of her books, and on the materials she had invented.

She alone had researched, developed, and promoted her work all over the world; the materials she used were specialized and expensive and her principles were high. As she saw it, other people had adopted her name and her approach to education simply to gain popularity and for financial reasons.

On the other hand, it was hard for others to believe that she was the only person who knew anything about the education of young children — and this was how she was often interpreted. What is certain is that, as one of her followers who left the movement said, the arguments set teachers whose interests were the same against each other, wasting energy in arguments among themselves instead of working together for the good of children.

The 1920s and 1930s — the twenty years between the two world wars — saw a great deal of interest in and discussion of education all over the world. This was partially because Maria Montessori and others had introduced new ideas. But it was also partially because, after the shock of World War I, there were hopes that better education would make people more tolerant of each other.

Also, the first twenty years of the twentieth century had brought huge changes in people's lives. Cars had become everyday sights. People no longer rushed outside to look if they heard an airplane. Electricity was bringing about a revolution in lighting and heating. Movies and sound recording — and, from the early 1920s on, radio — were major sources of entertainment. Many people thought that a method

"She was a fantastic personality. When she was around there was nothing else in the room. She seemed very motherly, very kind. She had beautiful dark eyes. We loved and respected her. To us she was next to God. She was vain, which amused us, but we loved her for that too."
Elise Braun Barnett,
one of Maria's
disciples in the 1920s

"Have you noticed what happens when you try to point out something to your dog? He does not look in the direction you are pointing, but at your outstretched hand and finger. I cannot help thinking that you are acting in a somewhat similar way in paying so much attention to me. . . . The highest honor and the deepest gratitude you can pay me is to turn your attention from me in the direction in which I am pointing — to The Child."
Maria Montessori, 1951

of education that dated from the days of the horse and cart could not be suitable for the exciting new age that had already begun.

Unpopularity

The Montessori Method, like other educational ideas, continued to be eagerly discussed and criticized. For some people Maria's ideas, despite all her talk of the love of children, were too coldly scientific.

One critic of Maria's methods, though not her goals, was A. S. Neill, who had founded Summerhill, an experimental school in England. Education, he said, was "more than matching colors and fitting cylinders into holes." One staff member who had taken the Montessori training course reported that Maria was a "frightful boss, terrible to her students."

Maria seems to have felt that the best thing to do was simply to avoid getting involved in arguments about her method. She rarely answered her critics. She could point to her successful Children's Houses in countries all over the world. Parents were eager to send their children to these schools and the children were just as eager to learn.

But in many ways it is unfortunate that Maria Montessori did not take part in the open discussion of education that went on in the 1920s and 1930s. Perhaps it was because she felt her name and method were being openly abused that she did not get involved in the debates that her work created. The praise followed closely by the criticism may have led to distrust. Maria chose to ignore it and to continue exactly as before, regardless of the often constructive criticism made of her.

Leaving Italy

Between the two world wars, there were more immediate troubles ahead for Maria. In 1922, the Fascist dictator Benito Mussolini took power in Italy. At first, things seemed to go well for Maria's movement. Mussolini promised her method his full support. Government money was provided for Montessori schools and a Montessori training college. Maria was made chief inspector of schools throughout Italy.

Mussolini was a politician. It suited him to have Italy's world-famous educator on his side. It suited Maria to have backing for her movement from a powerful government.

But the friendship did not last. By 1934, Mussolini's government was planning war against the African nation of Ethiopia and wanted to make Italian youth more aggressive and more primed for war. One way he thought he might accomplish this was to set up a Fascist youth organization. Members of this organization would wear uniforms at all times and give the Fascist salute.

When Mussolini insisted that children in Montessori schools join this organization, Maria broke with him. Many of the teachers directing schools according to her method were opposed to Mussolini's Fascist regime. In one day, all the Montessori schools in Italy closed, and shortly after that Maria decided to leave Italy and move to Spain.

Above: The Fascist dictator Benito Mussolini came to power in Italy in 1922. At first, his relationship with the Montessori movement was harmonious. Later, he began to interfere in Montessori schools. They were all closed overnight, and in 1934 Maria left Italy to settle in Spain.

Left: Maria's choice of Spain as her place of exile was an unfortunate one. Within two years, the Spanish Civil War had broken out, bringing terrible destruction to many of Spain's cities. Rival forces fought in the streets, and cities were bombed from the air.

Hard times

But it was a bad time for such a move.

Two years later, civil war broke out in Spain, and General Francisco Franco, another Fascist, took over. Maria was now sixty-six and desperate to find somewhere safe to settle down with her son Mario and her grandchildren. By this time Mario had joined her movement and acted as her "right-hand man," making arrangements for her lecture tours and acting as one of her translators, for she always lectured in Italian.

Bad luck seemed to follow Maria during the 1930s. She had had to leave her home country. Shortly after, when civil war broke out, she had to leave Spain, where she had hoped to settle. She was the founder of a worldwide movement, but she felt that the educational world did not give her the respect she deserved.

Her personal life was deeply unhappy. Mario had become her assistant, but she still would not acknowledge him in public as her son. So she introduced him as her nephew. To add to her unhappiness, Mario's marriage had broken up, and he had separated from his wife. Maria must have thought sometimes that although she was a recognized world expert on children, the child and grandchildren in her own life had not had easy lives.

Despite the interruptions to her life in the 1930s, Maria continued to lecture, although her ideas were perhaps taken less seriously. Her first books, such as *The Montessori Method* and *Dr. Montessori's Own Handbook*, began to look old-fashioned. Some of the people who had admired and followed her ideas in the early days had taken these ideas further. Among them was a Swiss educator, Jean Piaget, who was getting a lot of attention in the educational world.

Since 1935, Amsterdam, in Holland, had been the home — as it still is — of the International Montessori Association (AMI). Maria and Mario had founded the association in 1929 in Berlin.

After leaving Spain, Maria was offered a house in Holland, and she remained there from 1937 to 1939. It made good sense for her to live close to the headquarters of the movement she had started. But during the late thirties, this could have been

Mario Montessori, Maria's son, became her chief assistant and, after her death in 1952, took over leadership of the movement. It was only when her will was read after the funeral that Mario was publicly acknowledged as her son. In Maria's lifetime, he was described as her nephew.

dangerous. Had she been in Holland then, she would have had to make a quick escape when the Germans invaded in 1940.

Luckily, in 1939 she was invited to go to India.

India — a new beginning

There were already, in 1939, a number of Montessori schools in India. They had been founded by teachers who had been to Maria's training courses in Europe, and Maria was sure of a warm welcome there. Certainly it was clear that the war that broke out in Europe in September 1939 would be long and bitter. Maria, a lifelong lover of peace, left for India a month after the war began.

The journey itself was a challenge for a woman of nearly seventy. The flight from Holland was slow and cramped, and involved several overnight stops. In those days, only the most adventurous people flew, and wartime added to the dangers. Moreover, for people from Europe, the Indian climate is daunting.

But Maria arrived at the Madras airport full of energy and keen to start on her new work. Mentally, she was still alert, curious, and eager for new experiences, new people, and new places.

She could probably have made no better choice than India, where she was to stay for six years. More than any other people, Indians have great respect for the wisdom of elderly people. Moreover, Maria found her ideas about the "inner peace" present in every child to be deeply in tune with the Hindu religion that was, and is, practiced in India.

Maria found that a special village of palm-leaf huts had been built for her. It included a place for her to live, living quarters for her students, and a large lecture hut. Three hundred teachers and student teachers had signed up for her first course. They sat on the floor on rush mats while she lectured in Italian from a wicker armchair, with her son Mario acting as translator.

Before each day's lecture began, the students brought garlands of flowers which they placed around her neck, and set vases of fresh flowers on her table. The scene must have reminded Maria of the early days of her movement. After years of argument and

In India, during the years of World War II, Maria found an environment that suited her contemplative, mystic nature. As can be seen here, she adopted a version of Indian traditional dress. One writer, Rita Kramer, wrote of this period in Maria's life: "Now, towards the end of her life, she had found a place and a people eagerly waiting for her message and asking only to help her implement her ideas."

The Montessori ideal: a spacious, well-equipped classroom with children quietly absorbed in activities that they have chosen for themselves. Maria's critics doubted whether scenes like this were possible without the imposition of discipline from the teacher. Maria argued that the children's self-control came from their inner desires for order.

"She [Maria] liked it where there were friends. She was at home in India. The Indian girls were so lovely and they understood her and loved her and she needed that at the time. She felt she had been rejected in Europe and the United States, but in India every word of hers was soaked up. She was like a guru."

A friend of Maria Montessori, in India during the war years

of moving from one country to another, she was once again doing the thing she loved best — lecturing to an eager and enthusiastic audience. Her time in India was to be one of the happiest periods of her life.

The last years

Maria had intended to return to Holland in the summer of 1940, but by then Holland was under German occupation. Over the next six years, until after the war, she stayed in India and went thousands of miles to give lectures all over the country. After the war ended, she returned to Holland.

But still she did not rest. She was back in India in 1947, in Pakistan in 1949, touring through Europe in the same year, and in Austria in 1951; in 1952 she was

planning a lecture tour of Africa. She was never to take it. On May 6, 1952, at age eighty-one, she suddenly collapsed and died of a stroke.

The study at Maria's last home in Amsterdam, still the headquarters of AMI, is as busy as it was at the time of her death. On its walls are many souvenirs of her achievements, letters from students, medals and diplomas she had been awarded in countries all over the world, and photographs of her with her students and on grand occasions such as her presentation to the British royal court in London. On display are signed photographs from old friends and world leaders.

But the best record of Maria Montessori's life is not at 161 Koninginneweg, Amsterdam. It is in nursery schools and kindergartens, in children's

"To influence society we must turn our attention to childhood. Out of this truth comes the importance of nursery schools, for it is the little ones who are building our future, and they can work only on the materials we give them."
Maria Montessori, in
The Absorbent Mind

Opposite: Another photograph from Maria's 1951 visit to the Gatehouse School in London. One of Maria's gifts, which she showed from her earliest days at the first Casa dei Bambini, was an instant rapport with children. It is seen clearly here, where the children are gathering eagerly around to show her what they have done.

Below: To the end of her life, Maria liked nothing better than to spend a day with the children in a Montessori school. This picture was taken on her last visit to London in 1951.

playrooms, and even in toy shops all over the world. There is hardly anyone who has been to school in the past sixty years whose life has not been touched by Maria's ideas. And there are few young children in the world today who have not gained from the inspired teaching that began on that January morning in San Lorenzo, Rome, over eighty years ago.

Maria's vision of childhood

So what, nearly forty years after her death, has the world gained from the life of Maria Montessori?

First, we have gained a better understanding of what childhood is. Maria Montessori showed that children have a world of their own that has its own rules, and adults should not interfere. What is more, Maria believed, the child's world is a *better* world. Adults should learn from children instead of forcing children into adult ways of thinking. It is wrong to teach children without respecting their view of things.

Maria also spoke out in the public arena about the needs of children, taking her ideas beyond the classroom walls of teacher-educating institutions. She devoted time to the United Nations, providing insights about issues affecting children, and was involved in the International Year of the Child.

Third, Maria gave the world a better understanding of how children learn. They learn best at their own pace and in a happy atmosphere that allows them freedom to control their own activities.

But it is in the world around children that we can see the strongest influence of Maria Montessori: in the educational games, child-sized furniture, learning by discovery, bright classrooms, displays of interesting objects, teachers who take time to listen, and in so many of the ideas that are taught to students of teaching.

Maria Montessori was not always right. She would not listen to her critics and she would not alter her views in the light of new discoveries about the mind or about learning.

During her lifetime the world altered more than it had in all its previous history, but in 1950 she was still saying the same things, and telling the same stories, as she had forty years earlier.

58

Yet much of what she learned about children in the slums of Rome remains true enough to guide teachers in Montessori schools all over the world. And it lies, too, behind much of what goes on in almost all schools for young children, whether or not the teachers have heard her name. Maria liked to tell the story of a little girl who came for the first time to a Montessori school. The little girl is said to have asked the first child she met, "Is it true that in this school you're allowed to do what you like?"

"I don't know about that," replied the child after a pause, "but I do know that we like what we do!"

"Each of us has not always been a grown-up person. It was the child who instructed our personality."
    Maria Montessori, in
    The Absorbent Mind

For More Information . . .

Organizations

Write to the organizations listed below if you would like more information about subjects of interest to children, about education in America, and about Montessori schools. When you write, enclose a stamped envelope bearing your name and address so that they can use it when they write back to you. Be sure to explain exactly what you would like to know, and include your name, address, and age.

American Montessori Society
150 Fifth Avenue
New York, NY 10011

Children's Art Foundation
P.O. Box 83
Santa Cruz, CA 95063

Children's Film and Television Center
of America
School of Cinema/TV
University of Southern California
850 West 34th Street
Los Angeles, CA 90089

Children's Literature Association
Norma Bagnall, President
Missouri Western State College
Saint Joseph, MO 64507

Play Schools Association
19 West 44th Street
New York, NY 10036

For addresses of Montessori societies and training institutes all over the world . . .
Association Montessori Internationale
(AMI)
Koninginneweg 161, 1075 CN
Amsterdam, The Netherlands

Groups with special programs for children . . .
United Nations Children's Fund (UNICEF)
Beth Gragg, Dept. of Education
333 East 38th Street
New York, NY 10016

Save the Children Federation
54 Wilton Road
Westport, CT 06880

Magazines

The following magazines include articles about subjects that are interesting to children. These subjects include health, social problems, entertainment, science, and nature. Many of these magazines also have puzzles, games, projects, and suggestions for further reading. Check your local library or bookstore to see if they have these magazines or can order them for you.

Stone Soup: The Magazine by Children
Children's Art Foundation
P.O. Box 83
Santa Cruz, CA 95063

Cobblestone and *Faces*
20 Grove Street
Peterborough, NH 03458

Current Events and *Current Science*
Field Publications
P.O. Box 16626
Columbus, OH 43216

Current Health
P.O. Box 16504
Columbus, OH 43216

The Good Apple Newspaper
1204 Buchanan Street
P.O. Box 269
Carthage, IL 62321

Highlights for Children
2300 West Fifth Avenue
P.O. Box 269
Columbus, OH 43272

Junior Scholastic
2931 East McCarty Street
P.O. Box 3710
Jefferson City, MO 65102
. . . in Canada
Scholastic-TAB Publications, Ltd.
Richmond Hill, ON L4C 3G5 Canada

National Geographic
P.O. Box 2895
Washington, DC 20013

Books

The following books will give you more information about children, about education, and about Maria Montessori and her educational methods. Some of them are fiction, stories that take place in educational settings and that include children as the main characters. Check your library and bookstore to see if they have these books or can order them for you.

About Maria Montessori —

Maria Montessori: Her Life and Work. Standing (Penguin)
Montessori: A Modern Approach. Lilliard (Random House)

About children and education (fiction) —

Billy Bumbry's Year. Puffer (Lothrop, Lee & Shepard)
Don't Care High. Korman (Scholastic)
Jason. Hamilton (Herald Press)
Jonie Goes to Academy. Ritchie (Review & Herald)
Paddington Takes the Test. Bond (Houghton Mifflin)
The War Between the Pitiful Teachers and the Splendid Kids. Kiesel (Dutton)

About other issues of interest to children —

Every Kid's Guide to Understanding Human Rights. Berry (Childrens Press)
Your Future in Education. Milgram (Rosen Group)

Glossary

asylum
   A term formerly used to refer to an institution where people who are mentally or physically disabled might live. In Montessori's day conditions in asylums were poor and facilities were very basic. An asylum's main function was simply to keep residents away from society rather than help them fit into it.

Casa dei Bambini (The Children's House)
   The first Montessori school, started in San Lorenzo, a slum district of Rome, in 1907.

conference
A large meeting at which different speakers present lectures for the audience.

disciple
A close follower of any school of thought or leader or, perhaps, political movement; Maria Montessori's closest disciples were the women she allowed to call her "Mammolina," a term that is more personal than students would normally use when addressing their teachers or advisers.

elementary school
The level of school for children aged seven to eleven.

emancipation
The freeing from restraint, or restriction, of groups or individuals, especially in a social situation. This word has been used to refer to freeing slaves and to ensuring that women enjoy the same rights as men.

fascist
A term derived from the word *Fascisti*, which refers to a follower of dictator Benito Mussolini, before and during World War II. A fascist political party believes in the total power of the government headed by a dictator. Such a party stresses aggressive nationalism, or love for the home country, at the expense of some ethnic and national groups living in that country. It has a strong central government, usually at the expense of individual freedoms. The term is often used generally to refer to anyone who bullies or dictates to others.

feminism
The movement which campaigns for equal rights for women. Maria was a pioneering feminist because she fought to do things that had previously been done only by men; for example, she attended a boys' technical high school in order to study math, and she was the first woman in Italy to graduate from medical school.

Itard, Jean Marc Gaspard (1775-1838)
A doctor at a school in Paris for deaf children. He became famous for teaching the "Wild Boy of Aveyron." The "Wild Boy" had lived in the woods, surviving by living like an animal, for twelve years.

Kilpatrick, William Heard (1871-1965)
Director of the Columbia University Teacher's College, in New York City, in the early years of this century. Kilpatrick was a critic of Montessori.

Neill, A. S. (1883-1973)
British educational theorist who founded Summerhill School in Dorset in 1924. He found the Montessori method too restrictive, although he agreed with Maria's goals.

Piaget, Jean (1896-1980)
Swiss educator who was a supporter of Montessori in the 1920s and who himself became known internationally for his research on how children learn.

prejudice
Literally, to pre-judge; a judgement, especially an unfavorable one, which is based on inadequate knowledge.

private practice
    A form of medical practice in which doctors see patients in their own offices rather than in clinics or hospitals.

psychology
    The science that studies the mind — its states, emotions, and processes. Psychology helps us understand how people learn, think, and feel.

research
    Study to collect ideas on a subject, often leading to new ideas or discoveries.

retarded
    Literally "slowed down." A term used to describe people who, because of physical problems, learn at a much slower rate than others their age. In earlier years, children who were mentally retarded were often put in institutions. People did not believe they could learn what nondisabled children learned.

San Lorenzo
    A poor slum district in downtown Rome. It was here, in 1907, that Maria Montessori started her first Casa dei Bambini and that the Montessori movement began.

Seguin, Edouard (1811-80)
    A student of Itard's who specialized in the education of mentally retarded adults and children, first in Paris and later in the United States.

sensory learning materials
    The equipment used in the Montessori schools which was designed to teach the children through the senses: sight, sound, smell, taste, and touch. It was the basis of Maria's method of teaching and revolutionary in the education of children who had no disabilities.

special school
    A school especially for children with mental or physical disabilities. Called segregated sites in the United States, these are less common now as more schools avoid segregating disabled children, putting them instead in classes with those who have no disabilities.

technical school
    A school offering primarily science or technological subjects, such as computer science, carpentry, auto mechanics, engineering, and mathematics.

workhouse
    Also called a poorhouse; an institution where poor people who were physically able did unpaid work in return for food and lodging.

Chronology

1870   **August 31** — Maria Montessori is born at Chiaravalle, Ancona, Italy.

1875   Maria and her family move to Rome where, a year later, she starts school.

1882   Maria goes to a boys' school to study mathematics.

1886	Maria graduates from high school. She chooses to continue her education by attending a technical college.
1890	Maria begins a math and science course at the University of Rome.
1892	Maria, aged twenty-two, begins a course for a medical degree.
1896	**July 10** — Maria is awarded her degree as a doctor of medicine, becoming the first woman to graduate from the University of Rome's School of Medicine. **September** — Dr. Montessori goes to Berlin to speak at an international women's conference. **November** — She receives an appointment as a surgical assistant at Santo Spirilo Hospital, Rome.
1897	Maria speaks in Turin, Italy, at a national conference on children who are mentally retarded.
1898	Maria joins the National League for the Education of Retarded Children. At about this time, Maria falls in love with co-worker Giuseppe Montesano. **February** — Maria lectures in Milan, Padua, Venice, and Genoa on "The New Woman" and "Modern Charity."
1899	Maria is appointed as a lecturer at the women's teacher-training college and as a director of the State Orthophrenic School, in Rome, for children who are mentally retarded. She receives an award for outstanding service in hospitals. Maria lectures in Paris and London, where she is presented to Queen Victoria.
1901	Probable year of the birth of Mario, Montessori's son, whom the world believes to be her nephew until after her death. At age thirty-one, Maria returns to the University of Rome as a student of teaching, hygiene, and psychology.
1904	**December** — Maria is appointed as a lecturer in science and medicine at the University of Rome.
1907	**January 6** — Maria opens her first Children's House, Casa dei Bambini, in San Lorenzo, a suburb of Rome.
1909	**Summer** — The first Montessori training course is held at Citta di Castello.
1910	*The Montessori Method* is published. Shortly thereafter, Maria gives up her university post and hospital work to concentrate full time on lecturing, writing, and organizing.
1911	An American magazine, *McClure's*, publishes a long article about Montessori. By the end of the year, the first American Montessori school opens in New York. The Montessori Method becomes the standard system used in Italian and Swiss public schools.
1912	The first English translation of *The Montessori Method* appears. Many books by other authors attempting to explain or popularize Montessori's work begin to appear. Maria is dismayed.

1913   At age forty-three, Maria Montessori sets out on her first visit to the United States, where there are now over one hundred Montessori schools. The first Montessori school in Spain opens.

1914   *Dr. Montessori's Own Handbook* is published. America's leading educational theorist, William Heard Kilpatrick of Columbia University, attacks Montessori's ideas as outdated.

1915   Maria goes on her second and last tour of the United States, accompanied by her son Mario. She organizes a model Casa dei Bambini at the San Francisco world's fair with her disciple Helen Parkhurst as its teacher. Alexander Graham Bell becomes head of the Montessori Educational Association in America. Maria settles in Barcelona, Spain, her home for the next twenty years.

1915-17   The Montessori movement in America breaks up into quarreling factions.

1917   Maria's son, Mario, marries.

1918   Maria has a private audience with Pope Benedict XV, who orders that a complete set of her works be purchased by the Vatican Library.

1921-22   The Montessori Society of England undergoes turmoil and division.

1922   **Summer** — The first Children's House in Austria opens. Maria becomes an inspector of schools for the Italian government. **October** — Benito Mussolini takes power in Italy.

1924   **April** — Maria meets with Mussolini, who agrees to give her schools and movement official government support.

1929   The Association Montessori Internationale (AMI) is founded in Berlin to supervise the activities of Montessori schools and societies all over the world. The first International Montessori Congress is held at Elsinore in Denmark.

1934   Mussolini closes the Montessori schools in Italy. Maria leaves Italy and returns to live in Spain.

1935   The AMI moves to Amsterdam, where it has since remained.

1936   Maria Montessori leaves Spain and settles in Holland. She publishes *The Secret of Childhood.*

1939   **September** — World War II breaks out in Europe. **October** — Maria and Mario Montessori leave Holland to work in India. She is now sixty-nine years old.

1946   **July 30** — Maria returns to Amsterdam.

1947   Maria, at the age of seventy-six, undertakes a lecture tour in India which is to last two years.

1948   *What You Should Know About Your Child*, *The Discovery of the Child*, and *To Educate the Human Potential* are published.

Classrooms such as this are designed for the child. The furniture is scaled for children, the walls contain their artwork, and the children can move about quite freely. Before Montessori, teachers had thought primarily about the subjects they would teach the children, not their comfort and special educational needs.

1949   Maria visits Pakistan, Italy, France, Austria, Britain, and Ireland. She publishes *The Absorbent Mind* and is nominated for the Nobel Peace Prize.

1950   At age seventy-nine, Maria gives lecture tours in Norway and Sweden and is again nominated for the Nobel Peace Prize.
June — Montessori speaks at a United Nations education conference in Florence, Italy.

1951   Maria is nominated for the Nobel Peace Prize for the third and final time.
July — Maria runs a training course at Innsbruck, Austria.

1952   **May 6** — At the age of eighty-one, Maria Montessori collapses and dies at Noordwijk aan Zee, in Holland.

1990   The AMI records over 130 approved Montessori schools in the United States alone. There are also at least four thousand nonapproved "Montessori" schools that use part of her method in their educational programs.

Index